A YEAR OF *adventure*

Toby the fire dog

BOOK-2

Written by David Bannister

Toby's Adventures

Toby The Fire Dog

Book-2

The Gate is left open

Toby sat in the garden watching the butterflies and bees flying by.

It was a fine summer day.

The garden gate was lying open again.

"I wonder if there will be any adventures today?" thought Toby.

It wasn't long until Toby's nose started to twitch. Sniff sniff.

"What is that smell?" he said to himself. Then he noticed a puff of smoke floating past.

"Now where did that come from?" he thought.

His senses told him something wasn't right, so Toby was about to begin another adventure.

Toby put his nose in the air and got a whiff of the smoke smell again.

He started to follow the smell which led him to the forest. He noticed two boys who were up to some sort of mischief.

Toby gave the boys a couple of loud barks.

The boys just laughed at Toby and ran away, leaving Toby with the mischief they were up to.

Toby knew something dangerous was going to happen. He knew he had to get help.

But how?

He started to run home as fast as he could.

On his way home he noticed a fire station.

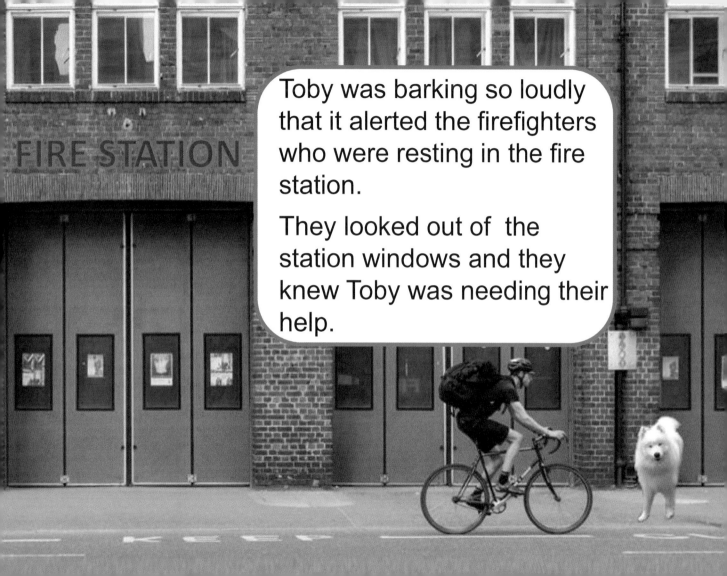

Toby was barking so loudly that it alerted the firefighters who were resting in the fire station.

They looked out of the station windows and they knew Toby was needing their help.

Toby had barked so much to get help and was panting so fast, the fire chief could not make him out.

"What's wrong?" The Fire Chief asked Toby. Toby woof woofed the whole story again.

The firefighters started getting ready. They already had their trousers and boots on, so they only needed their jacket and gloves to protect their body and hands. They also needed their face and head protection.

Within minutes the fire station doors were open and the fire engine was heading down the street with Toby on board.

The firefighters finished getting dressed in the fire engine.

Toby was enjoying the ride on the big fire engine with its siren beating out;
Nee Nah, Nee Nah.

It didn't take long to get there as Toby was Woof woofing the directions.

The fire engine raced into the forest.

The fire was getting out of control!

The fire engine pulled into the forest carpark. The firefighters jumped out. Toby joined them and watched as they connected up the water hoses. The firefighters headed over to the fire and didn't take long to put it out.

The fire was out now and the forest had been saved.

The firefighters said it was saved because of Toby's quick action.

Toby sat by the fire engine as the men put all the gear back into it.

Toby watched as all the equipment was put back into place.

It was so tidy and organised.

All the fire hoses were rolled up and secured back into the Fire engine. The covers were then closed and the fire engine was ready to return to the fire station.

Toby arrived back at his garden and all he wanted to do after getting a drink, was to put his head down and have a snooze. Before Toby got over to sleep, he was startled by the big fire engine pulling up outside his gate.

Toby's award for his bravery was a medal which he wore with pride. He also was given a large cup.

But Toby's favorite award was his very own number one fire fighter hat.

Toby was wearing his medal as he was driven around his home town to show it off.

Toby also got to inspect all the fire engines in the fire station.

The End

David Bannister